Marketing 101

Utilizing the Basics in Marketing

Daniel A. Garcia

Dedication

This is dedicated to all of those involved - in the diverse world of marketing.

Dedicated to Professor Laura De La Cruz and Professor Susan Williams. Two outstanding instructors in Business and Marketing. Thank You!

Go Get 'EM!

How to Use

This journal is made up of the following:

- Check list: To check off questions/tips. Gives a visual of progress made, in this particular journal.
- Note section: To make note of activity.

Divided into five (5) sections:

- Strategic planning.
- Target market.
- The four P's.
- Research.
- Goals – short-term & long-term.

Strategic Planning

Marketing is a very diverse, complex and overall, a fun subject. But, it all begins with some planning. A plan is only as good - as those seeing it through – in its entire duration. It's a good trait or habit to write down certain objectives and/or goals. This section is geared towards this concept.

The following section contains:

- Header: to write down idea or plan, along with the date.
- Check list: to give a physical check list, to check off questions.
- Questions: to assist the planning process, by asking critical questions.
- Note section: to make note of activity.

Plan Objective: _____ Date: _____

❑ What is the plan? Why should I go through with this plan? Is it achievable?

_____
_____
_____
_____
_____

❑ What is the duration, of this plan? Is it a short-term or long-term plan?

_____
_____
_____
_____
_____

❑ What raw materials do I need? What are some of the costs? Will this be profitable?

_____
_____
_____
_____
_____

❑ What are the pros and cons of this idea? What is the cause and effect?

_____
_____
_____
_____

Plan Objective: _____ Date: _____

❑ What is the plan? Why should I go through with this plan? Is it achievable?

_____
_____
_____
_____
_____

❑ What is the duration, of this plan? Is it a short-term or long-term plan?

_____
_____
_____
_____

❑ What raw materials do I need? What are some of the costs? Will this be profitable?

_____
_____
_____
_____
_____

❑ What are the pros and cons of this idea? What is the cause and effect?

_____
_____
_____
_____

Plan Objective: _____ Date: _____

☐ What is the plan? Why should I go through with this plan? Is it achievable?

_____
_____
_____
_____
_____

☐ What is the duration, of this plan? Is it a short-term or long-term plan?

_____
_____
_____
_____
_____

☐ What raw materials do I need? What are some of the costs? Will this be profitable?

_____
_____
_____
_____
_____

☐ What are the pros and cons of this idea? What is the cause and effect?

_____
_____
_____
_____

Plan Objective: _____ Date: _____

❑ What is the plan? Why should I go through with this plan? Is it achievable?

_____

_____

_____

_____

_____

❑ What is the duration, of this plan? Is it a short-term or long-term plan?

_____

_____

_____

_____

_____

❑ What raw materials do I need? What are some of the costs? Will this be profitable?

_____

_____

_____

_____

_____

❑ What are the pros and cons of this idea? What is the cause and effect?

_____

_____

_____

_____

Plan Objective: _____ Date: _____

❑ What is the plan? Why should I go through with this plan? Is it achievable?

_____

_____

_____

_____

_____

❑ What is the duration, of this plan? Is it a short-term or long-term plan?

_____

_____

_____

_____

_____

❑ What raw materials do I need? What are some of the costs? Will this be profitable?

_____

_____

_____

_____

_____

❑ What are the pros and cons of this idea? What is the cause and effect?

_____

_____

_____

_____

Plan Objective: _____ Date: _____

❑ What is the plan? Why should I go through with this plan? Is it achievable?

_____
_____
_____
_____
_____

❑ What is the duration, of this plan? Is it a short-term or long-term plan?

_____
_____
_____
_____
_____

❑ What raw materials do I need? What are some of the costs? Will this be profitable?

_____
_____
_____
_____
_____

❑ What are the pros and cons of this idea? What is the cause and effect?

_____
_____
_____
_____

Plan Objective: _____ Date: _____

❑ What is the plan? Why should I go through with this plan? Is it achievable?

_____
_____
_____
_____
_____

❑ What is the duration, of this plan? Is it a short-term or long-term plan?

_____
_____
_____
_____
_____

❑ What raw materials do I need? What are some of the costs? Will this be profitable?

_____
_____
_____
_____
_____

❑ What are the pros and cons of this idea? What is the cause and effect?

_____
_____
_____
_____

Plan Objective: _____ Date: _____

☐ What is the plan? Why should I go through with this plan? Is it achievable?

_____
_____
_____
_____
_____

☐ What is the duration, of this plan? Is it a short-term or long-term plan?

_____
_____
_____
_____
_____

☐ What raw materials do I need? What are some of the costs? Will this be profitable?

_____
_____
_____
_____
_____

☐ What are the pros and cons of this idea? What is the cause and effect?

_____
_____
_____
_____

Target Market

Finding your target market/audience, is a very critical step – in marketing. "Everyone" is **<u>NOT</u>** your target market. So, every business needs to keep this in mind. In regards to finding your specific demographic/niche. This really makes room for specialization. Which would mean, a respective business, developing their strengths to their fullest extent.

<u>The following section contains:</u>
- Header: to write down target market (men, women, teenagers, etc).
- Check list: to give a physical check list, to check off questions.
- Questions: to assist the planning process, by asking critical questions.
- Note section: to make note of activity.

Target Market: _____ Date: _____

❑ Who is your target market? Is there more than one?

_____
_____
_____
_____
_____

❑ How do you plan to reach them? How are you going to build a strong – customer loyalty?

_____
_____
_____
_____
_____

❑ Will you advertise? What ads will make up your campaign? Social media, print, billboard ads?

_____
_____
_____
_____
_____

❑ Are you getting any feedback? Do you offer surveys, either online or in person (hardcopy)?

_____
_____
_____
_____

Target Market: _____ Date: _____

❑ Who is your target market? Is there more than one?

_____
_____
_____
_____
_____

❑ How do you plan to reach them? How are you going to build a strong – customer loyalty?

_____
_____
_____
_____
_____

❑ Will you advertise? What ads will make up your campaign? Social media, print, billboard ads?

_____
_____
_____
_____
_____

❑ Are you getting any feedback? Do you offer surveys, either online or in person (hardcopy)?

_____
_____
_____
_____

Target Market: _____ Date: _____

❑ Who is your target market? Is there more than one?

_____

_____

_____

_____

_____

❑ How do you plan to reach them? How are you going to build a strong – customer loyalty?

_____

_____

_____

_____

_____

❑ Will you advertise? What ads will make up your campaign? Social media, print, billboard ads?

_____

_____

_____

_____

_____

❑ Are you getting any feedback? Do you offer surveys, either online or in person (hardcopy)?

_____

_____

_____

_____

Target Market: _____ Date: _____

❑ Who is your target market? Is there more than one?

_____

_____

_____

_____

_____

❑ How do you plan to reach them? How are you going to build a strong – customer loyalty?

_____

_____

_____

_____

❑ Will you advertise? What ads will make up your campaign? Social media, print, billboard ads?

_____

_____

_____

_____

❑ Are you getting any feedback? Do you offer surveys, either online or in person (hardcopy)?

_____

_____

_____

_____

Target Market: _____ Date: _____

❑ Who is your target market? Is there more than one?

_____

_____

_____

_____

_____

❑ How do you plan to reach them? How are you going to build a strong – customer loyalty?

_____

_____

_____

_____

❑ Will you advertise? What ads will make up your campaign? Social media, print, billboard ads?

_____

_____

_____

_____

_____

❑ Are you getting any feedback? Do you offer surveys, either online or in person (hardcopy)?

_____

_____

_____

_____

Target Market: _____ Date: _____

☐ Who is your target market? Is there more than one?

_____
_____
_____
_____
_____

☐ How do you plan to reach them? How are you going to build a strong – customer loyalty?

_____
_____
_____
_____

☐ Will you advertise? What ads will make up your campaign? Social media, print, billboard ads?

_____
_____
_____
_____
_____

☐ Are you getting any feedback? Do you offer surveys, either online or in person (hardcopy)?

_____
_____
_____
_____

Target Market: _____ Date: _____

❑ Who is your target market? Is there more than one?

_____

_____

_____

_____

_____

❑ How do you plan to reach them? How are you going to build a strong – customer loyalty?

_____

_____

_____

_____

_____

❑ Will you advertise? What ads will make up your campaign? Social media, print, billboard ads?

_____

_____

_____

_____

_____

❑ Are you getting any feedback? Do you offer surveys, either online or in person (hardcopy)?

_____

_____

_____

Target Market: _____ Date: _____

❑ Who is your target market? Is there more than one?

_____

_____

_____

_____

_____

❑ How do you plan to reach them? How are you going to build a strong – customer loyalty?

_____

_____

_____

_____

_____

❑ Will you advertise? What ads will make up your campaign? Social media, print, billboard ads?

_____

_____

_____

_____

_____

❑ Are you getting any feedback? Do you offer surveys, either online or in person (hardcopy)?

_____

_____

_____

_____

The Four P's

The four P's in marketing, are made up of the following - *product*, *price*, *promotion* and *placement*. It's important to have an understanding of these elements. And even more important and critical to use them.

The following section contains:

- Header: to list the product, price, promotion and place.
- Check list: to give a physical check list, to check off questions.
- Questions: to assist the planning process, by asking critical questions.
- Note section: to make note of activity.

➢ There are five slots, for five products.

Name of Product: _____ Date: _____

❑ What is your product? What can it do? Or why
   should consumers, purchase your product?

_____
_____
_____
_____
_____

❑ How new or old is your product? Is there a plan
   in place - to revise it? As the years go by?

_____
_____
_____
_____
_____

❑ Is your product available at your physical retail
   location? Online? Or both?

_____
_____
_____
_____
_____

❑ How happy, are customer? With your product(s)?
   What reviews have you received?

_____
_____
_____
_____

List your Price: $_____._____ Date: _____

❑ How much does it cost to build your product?
What vendors (if any) are carried in your store?

_____
_____
_____
_____
_____

❑ Have you priced matched with your competitors?
Are your able to beat your competition?

_____
_____
_____
_____
_____

❑ Is your price modest? What markdowns/markups
have you done in the past six months?

_____
_____
_____
_____
_____

❑ Are you breaking even/reaping a good profit? Or
losing money? What can you do, to save money?

_____
_____
_____
_____

Promotion: _____ Date: _____

❑ Have you come up with some ideas/plans for promotion? What are they?

_____
_____
_____
_____
_____

❑ Will you be doing any special sales? Such as, buy x-amount, get x-amount free?

_____
_____
_____
_____
_____

❑ Do you have a website? Is there a page, where customers can see the latest?

_____
_____
_____
_____
_____

❑ Are you using social media? Is this free channel of advertisement/availability; linked to your website?

_____
_____
_____
_____

Placement:_____   Date:_____

❑ Where is your product placed? In a physical retail
  space - store rack? Or Online?

_____

_____

_____

_____

_____

❑ What product(s) receive the most attention
  (traffic)? Are those on display – in clear sight?

_____

_____

_____

_____

_____

❑ How accessible are your products? Can
  customers find things with ease?

_____

_____

_____

_____

_____

❑ How happy/satisfied are your consumers? Are
  you ceasing to their dollar votes?

_____

_____

_____

_____

Name of Product: _____ Date: _____

❑ What is your product? What can it do? Or why should consumers, purchase your product?

_____
_____
_____
_____
_____

❑ How new or old is your product? Is there a plan in place - to revise it? As the years go by?

_____
_____
_____
_____
_____

❑ Is your product available at your physical retail location? Online? Or both?

_____
_____
_____
_____
_____

❑ How happy, are customer? With your product(s)? What reviews have you received?

_____
_____
_____
_____

List your Price: $_____._____ Date: _____

❏ How much does it cost to build your product?
   What vendors (if any) are carried in your store?

_____
_____
_____
_____
_____

❏ Have you priced matched with your competitors?
   Are your able to beat your competition?

_____
_____
_____
_____

❏ Is your price modest? What markdowns/markups
   have you done in the past six months?

_____
_____
_____
_____

❏ Are you breaking even/reaping a good profit? Or
   losing money? What can you do, to save money?

_____
_____
_____

Promotion:_____   Date: _____

❑ Have you come up with some ideas/plans for promotion? What are they?

_____
_____
_____
_____
_____

❑ Will you be doing any special sales? Such as, buy x-amount, get x-amount free?

_____
_____
_____
_____
_____

❑ Do you have a website? Is there a page, where customers can see the latest?

_____
_____
_____
_____
_____

❑ Are you using social media? Is this free channel of advertisement/availability; linked to your website?

_____
_____
_____
_____

Placement: _____ Date: _____

❑ Where is your product placed? In a physical retail
space - store rack? Or Online?

_____
_____
_____
_____
_____

❑ What product(s) receive the most attention
(traffic)? Are those on display – in clear sight?

_____
_____
_____
_____

❑ How accessible are your products? Can
customers find things with ease?

_____
_____
_____
_____

❑ How happy/satisfied are your consumers? Are
you ceasing to their dollar votes?

_____
_____
_____
_____

Name of Product: _____ Date: _____

❑ What is your product? What can it do? Or why
   should consumers, purchase your product?

   _____
   _____
   _____
   _____
   _____

❑ How new or old is your product? Is there a plan
   in place - to revise it? As the years go by?

   _____
   _____
   _____
   _____

❑ Is your product available at your physical retail
   location? Online? Or both?

   _____
   _____
   _____
   _____
   _____

❑ How happy, are customer? With your product(s)?
   What reviews have you received?

   _____
   _____
   _____
   _____

List your Price: $_____ . _____ Date: _____

❑ How much does it cost to build your product?
What vendors (if any) are carried in your store?

_____
_____
_____
_____
_____

❑ Have you priced matched with your competitors?
Are your able to beat your competition?

_____
_____
_____
_____
_____

❑ Is your price modest? What markdowns/markups
have you done in the past six months?

_____
_____
_____
_____
_____

❑ Are you breaking even/reaping a good profit? Or
losing money? What can you do, to save money?

_____
_____
_____
_____

Promotion: _____   Date: _____

❑ Have you come up with some ideas/plans for promotion? What are they?

_____
_____
_____
_____
_____

❑ Will you be doing any special sales? Such as, buy x-amount, get x-amount free?

_____
_____
_____
_____
_____

❑ Do you have a website? Is there a page, where customers can see the latest?

_____
_____
_____
_____
_____

❑ Are you using social media? Is this free channel of advertisement/availability; linked to your website?

_____
_____
_____
_____

Placement:_____   Date:_____

❑ Where is your product placed? In a physical retail
 space - store rack? Or Online?

_____

_____

_____

_____

_____

❑ What product(s) receive the most attention
 (traffic)? Are those on display – in clear sight?

_____

_____

_____

_____

_____

❑ How accessible are your products? Can
 customers find things with ease?

_____

_____

_____

_____

_____

❑ How happy/satisfied are your consumers? Are
 you ceasing to their dollar votes?

_____

_____

_____

_____

Name of Product: _____ Date: _____

❑ What is your product? What can it do? Or why
   should consumers, purchase your product?

   _____

   _____

   _____

   _____

   _____

❑ How new or old is your product? Is there a plan
   in place - to revise it? As the years go by?

   _____

   _____

   _____

   _____

   _____

❑ Is your product available at your physical retail
   location? Online? Or both?

   _____

   _____

   _____

   _____

   _____

❑ How happy, are customer? With your product(s)?
   What reviews have you received?

   _____

   _____

   _____

   _____

List your Price: $_____._____ Date: _____

❑ How much does it cost to build your product?
What vendors (if any) are carried in your store?

_____
_____
_____
_____
_____

❑ Have you priced matched with your competitors?
Are your able to beat your competition?

_____
_____
_____
_____
_____

❑ Is your price modest? What markdowns/markups
have you done in the past six months?

_____
_____
_____
_____
_____

❑ Are you breaking even/reaping a good profit? Or
losing money? What can you do, to save money?

_____
_____
_____
_____

Promotion: _____　　Date: _____

❑ Have you come up with some ideas/plans for promotion? What are they?

_____
_____
_____
_____
_____

❑ Will you be doing any special sales? Such as, buy x-amount, get x-amount free?

_____
_____
_____
_____
_____

❑ Do you have a website? Is there a page, where customers can see the latest?

_____
_____
_____
_____
_____

❑ Are you using social media? Is this free channel of advertisement/availability; linked to your website?

_____
_____
_____
_____

Placement:_____   Date:_____

❑ Where is your product placed? In a physical retail
  space - store rack? Or Online?

_____

_____

_____

_____

_____

❑ What product(s) receive the most attention
  (traffic)? Are those on display – in clear sight?

_____

_____

_____

_____

_____

❑ How accessible are your products? Can
  customers find things with ease?

_____

_____

_____

_____

_____

❑ How happy/satisfied are your consumers? Are
  you ceasing to their dollar votes?

_____

_____

_____

_____

Name of Product: _____ Date: _____

❑ What is your product? What can it do? Or why should consumers, purchase your product?

_____
_____
_____
_____
_____

❑ How new or old is your product? Is there a plan in place - to revise it? As the years go by?

_____
_____
_____
_____
_____

❑ Is your product available at your physical retail location? Online? Or both?

_____
_____
_____
_____
_____

❑ How happy, are customer? With your product(s)? What reviews have you received?

_____
_____
_____
_____

List your Price: $_____ . _____ Date: _____

❑ How much does it cost to build your product?
   What vendors (if any) are carried in your store?

_____

_____

_____

_____

_____

❑ Have you priced matched with your competitors?
   Are your able to beat your competition?

_____

_____

_____

_____

❑ Is your price modest? What markdowns/markups
   have you done in the past six months?

_____

_____

_____

_____

❑ Are you breaking even/reaping a good profit? Or
   losing money? What can you do, to save money?

_____

_____

_____

Promotion: _____ Date: _____

❑ Have you come up with some ideas/plans for promotion? What are they?

_____
_____
_____
_____
_____

❑ Will you be doing any special sales? Such as, buy x-amount, get x-amount free?

_____
_____
_____
_____
_____

❑ Do you have a website? Is there a page, where customers can see the latest?

_____
_____
_____
_____
_____

❑ Are you using social media? Is this free channel of advertisement/availability; linked to your website?

_____
_____
_____
_____

Placement:_____   Date:_____

❏ Where is your product placed? In a physical retail space - store rack? Or Online?

_____
_____
_____
_____
_____

❏ What product(s) receive the most attention (traffic)? Are those on display – in clear sight?

_____
_____
_____
_____

❏ How accessible are your products? Can customers find things with ease?

_____
_____
_____
_____
_____

❏ How happy/satisfied are your consumers? Are you ceasing to their dollar votes?

_____
_____
_____
_____

Research

Research – will pay off in due time. Research is vitally important for any professional endeavor(s). This means "doing your homework". In Marketing, one needs to know - what they are working with. In this section, the layout will help in your research – with geographic, demographic and psychographic.

The following section contains:
- Header: to write research attempt and date.
- Check list: to give a physical check list, to check off questions.
- Questions: to assist the planning process, by asking critical questions.
- Note section: to make note of activity.

Research Attempt: # _____   Date: _____

❑ Have you researched - the geographical area?
Customer wants, given the location?

_____
_____
_____
_____
_____

❑ How are you reaching your demographic? How
will you market based on age, education, income?

_____
_____
_____
_____
_____

❑ Have you studied/researched people's buying
habits/behaviors? Given psychographic factors?

_____
_____
_____
_____
_____

❑ Have you been able to fuse all geographic,
demographic and psychographic factors?

_____
_____
_____
_____

Research Attempt: #_____   Date:_____

❏ Have you researched - the geographical area?
   Customer wants, given the location?

_____
_____
_____
_____
_____

❏ How are you reaching your demographic? How
   will you market based on age, education, income?

_____
_____
_____
_____
_____

❏ Have you studied/researched people's buying
   habits/behaviors? Given psychographic factors?

_____
_____
_____
_____
_____

❏ Have you been able to fuse all geographic,
   demographic and psychographic factors?

_____
_____
_____
_____

Research Attempt: #_____   Date:_____

❑ Have you researched - the geographical area?
   Customer wants, given the location?

_____
_____
_____
_____
_____

❑ How are you reaching your demographic? How
   will you market based on age, education, income?

_____
_____
_____
_____
_____

❑ Have you studied/researched people's buying
   habits/behaviors? Given psychographic factors?

_____
_____
_____
_____
_____

❑ Have you been able to fuse all geographic,
   demographic and psychographic factors?

_____
_____
_____
_____

Research Attempt: #_____   Date:_____

☐ Have you researched - the geographical area?
  Customer wants, given the location?

_____
_____
_____
_____
_____

☐ How are you reaching your demographic? How
  will you market based on age, education, income?

_____
_____
_____
_____
_____

☐ Have you studied/researched people's buying
  habits/behaviors? Given psychographic factors?

_____
_____
_____
_____
_____

☐ Have you been able to fuse all geographic,
  demographic and psychographic factors?

_____
_____
_____
_____

Research Attempt: #_____   Date:_____

❑ Have you researched - the geographical area?
   Customer wants, given the location?

_____
_____
_____
_____
_____

❑ How are you reaching your demographic? How
   will you market based on age, education, income?

_____
_____
_____
_____
_____

❑ Have you studied/researched people's buying
   habits/behaviors? Given psychographic factors?

_____
_____
_____
_____
_____

❑ Have you been able to fuse all geographic,
   demographic and psychographic factors?

_____
_____
_____
_____

Research Attempt: #_____   Date: _____

❑ Have you researched - the geographical area?
  Customer wants, given the location?

_____
_____
_____
_____
_____

❑ How are you reaching your demographic? How
  will you market based on age, education, income?

_____
_____
_____
_____
_____

❑ Have you studied/researched people's buying
  habits/behaviors? Given psychographic factors?

_____
_____
_____
_____
_____

❑ Have you been able to fuse all geographic,
  demographic and psychographic factors?

_____
_____
_____

Research Attempt: #_____   Date:_____

❑ Have you researched - the geographical area?
   Customer wants, given the location?

_____
_____
_____
_____
_____

❑ How are you reaching your demographic? How
   will you market based on age, education, income?

_____
_____
_____
_____

❑ Have you studied/researched people's buying
   habits/behaviors? Given psychographic factors?

_____
_____
_____
_____

❑ Have you been able to fuse all geographic,
   demographic and psychographic factors?

_____
_____
_____

Research Attempt: #_____   Date:_____

❑ Have you researched - the geographical area?
   Customer wants, given the location?

_____
_____
_____
_____
_____

❑ How are you reaching your demographic? How
   will you market based on age, education, income?

_____
_____
_____
_____

❑ Have you studied/researched people's buying
   habits/behaviors? Given psychographic factors?

_____
_____
_____
_____
_____

❑ Have you been able to fuse all geographic,
   demographic and psychographic factors?

_____
_____
_____
_____

Goals – Short-term/Long-term

Having good, well thought-out goals are always a plus. It's good to make life - based on goals both short-term and long-term; both personally and professionally.

The following section contains:
- Header: to write out goal and date.
- Check list: to give a physical check list, to check off questions.
- Questions: to assist the planning process, by asking critical questions.
- Note section: to make note of activity.

Goal: _____ Date: _____

❏ What is your short-term goal? Will it be
   accomplished within days? Weeks? Months?

_____

_____

_____

_____

_____

❏ How will this short-term goal play out? Will it
   reap positive benefits? Or negative consequences?

_____

_____

_____

_____

_____

❏ What are some long-term goals? Will you
   accomplish them in months, years, five years?

_____

_____

_____

_____

_____

❏ What is your desired outcome? Is your long-term
   realistic enough, for achievement?

_____

_____

_____

_____

Goal: _____ Date: _____

❑ What is your short-term goal? Will it be
   accomplished within days? Weeks? Months?

_____

_____

_____

_____

_____

❑ How will this short-term goal play out? Will it
   reap positive benefits? Or negative consequences?

_____

_____

_____

_____

_____

❑ What are some long-term goals? Will you
   accomplish them in months, years, five years?

_____

_____

_____

_____

_____

❑ What is your desired outcome? Is your long-term
   realistic enough, for achievement?

_____

_____

_____

_____

Goal: _____ Date: _____

❑ What is your short-term goal? Will it be
   accomplished within days? Weeks? Months?

_____

_____

_____

_____

_____

❑ How will this short-term goal play out? Will it
   reap positive benefits? Or negative consequences?

_____

_____

_____

_____

_____

❑ What are some long-term goals? Will you
   accomplish them in months, years, five years?

_____

_____

_____

_____

_____

❑ What is your desired outcome? Is your long-term
   realistic enough, for achievement?

_____

_____

_____

_____

Goal: _____ Date: _____

❑ What is your short-term goal? Will it be
   accomplished within days? Weeks? Months?

_____
_____
_____
_____
_____

❑ How will this short-term goal play out? Will it
   reap positive benefits? Or negative consequences?

_____
_____
_____
_____
_____

❑ What are some long-term goals? Will you
   accomplish them in months, years, five years?

_____
_____
_____
_____
_____

❑ What is your desired outcome? Is your long-term
   realistic enough, for achievement?

_____
_____
_____
_____

Goal: _____ Date: _____

❑ What is your short-term goal? Will it be
   accomplished within days? Weeks? Months?

_____
_____
_____
_____
_____

❑ How will this short-term goal play out? Will it
   reap positive benefits? Or negative consequences?

_____
_____
_____
_____
_____

❑ What are some long-term goals? Will you
   accomplish them in months, years, five years?

_____
_____
_____
_____
_____

❑ What is your desired outcome? Is your long-term
   realistic enough, for achievement?

_____
_____
_____
_____

Goal: _____ Date: _____

❑ What is your short-term goal? Will it be
  accomplished within days? Weeks? Months?

_____
_____
_____
_____
_____

❑ How will this short-term goal play out? Will it
  reap positive benefits? Or negative consequences?

_____
_____
_____
_____
_____

❑ What are some long-term goals? Will you
  accomplish them in months, years, five years?

_____
_____
_____
_____
_____

❑ What is your desired outcome? Is your long-term
  realistic enough, for achievement?

_____
_____
_____
_____

Goal: _____ Date: _____

❑ What is your short-term goal? Will it be
   accomplished within days? Weeks? Months?

_____

_____

_____

_____

_____

❑ How will this short-term goal play out? Will it
   reap positive benefits? Or negative consequences?

_____

_____

_____

_____

_____

❑ What are some long-term goals? Will you
   accomplish them in months, years, five years?

_____

_____

_____

_____

_____

❑ What is your desired outcome? Is your long-term
   realistic enough, for achievement?

_____

_____

_____

_____

Goal: _____ Date: _____

❑ What is your short-term goal? Will it be
   accomplished within days? Weeks? Months?

_____
_____
_____
_____
_____

❑ How will this short-term goal play out? Will it
   reap positive benefits? Or negative consequences?

_____
_____
_____
_____
_____

❑ What are some long-term goals? Will you
   accomplish them in months, years, five years?

_____
_____
_____
_____
_____

❑ What is your desired outcome? Is your long-term
   realistic enough, for achievement?

_____
_____
_____
_____

Marketing surly is an intensive, innovated, complex and overall – a fun subject. My hat goes off to all of those working in the field. This is a study that is always evolving.

Thank you, for purchasing this journal. Please keep a look out for more; and feel free to leave your review.

Best Wishes,
Daniel A. Garcia